salmonpoetry

Publishing Irish & International
Poetry Since 1981

the arts council
an chomhairle
ealaíon

funding
literature
artscouncil.ie

Fox Trousers

Eithne Hand

Published in 2020 by
Salmon Poetry
Cliffs of Moher, County Clare, Ireland
Website: www.salmonpoetry.com
Email: info@salmonpoetry.com

ISBN 978-1-912561-92-6

Cover Image: © *Roeselien Raimond www.roeselienraimond.com*
Cover Design & Typesetting: *Siobhán Hutson*

Printed in Ireland by Sprint Print

*Salmon Poetry gratefully acknowledges the support of
The Arts Council / An Chomhairle Ealaíon*

Acknowledgements

My thanks to the editors of the following publications where some of these poems first appeared:

THE SHOp, Stony Thursday, Southword, Crannóg, The Irish Times, The Cormorant, The Moth and Poetry Ireland Review. A version of this collection was shortlisted for the Patrick Kavanagh Poetry Award.

"The End of St. Barbara" was highly commended in the Gregory O'Donoghue International competition in 2016, "Air Brakes" was shortlisted for the Fish Poetry Prize 2018 and "Clearing the Lane" for the Fish Poetry Prize 2020.

I would like to thank Wicklow County Council, Words Ireland and Poetry Ireland for their support through the Wicklow Literature Mentoring Scheme in 2016. Thanks also to the Tyrone Guthrie Centre, Annaghmakerrig, Co. Monaghan, where some of these poems were written.

Special thanks to my endlessly supportive poetry friends, especially Jane Clarke, Jessica Traynor, Rosamund Taylor, Liam Thompson, Richard Cox, Grace Wells, Katie Donovan, James Harpur, the Hunters Poetry Reading Group and the late Shirley McClure.

None of this work would have been possible without the initial encouragement of Catherine Phil MacCarthy.

My gratitude to my family, past and present, for their inspiration and to Mikel Murfi for his love.

Contents

for Máire Tobin and Des Hand

Summer Yearn

It's almost dark in my bedroom,
outside the lake still glows.
If I could just slide from these covers
and lie in the tickling grass,
I'd eavesdrop on the crowd
readying for the night –
pulling on their fox trousers, badger coats,
heading for our neighbours' hills.
Hares on the beat, hedgehogs on the ball,
deer drinking long in the late night lake-bar.
Mink slink through brambles
as midnight's satin shifts from the east,
and a liquid dark slips over us all.

Attention

A lot of men hold on to their penises
while they sleep, she said.

At once all men in the class
crossed legs or removed hands
from pockets as women smiled

and recognised the sight,
the return to little boydom
that comes in deep subconscious,

protecting, caressing,
making sure it's still there.
Still. There. The look is

comforting, vulnerable.
No armour now
of over and underwear,

just a hand curled
around their jewels
like an oyster shell.

Hard Chaw

Harry was her fellah
but only cos she said so.

Too scared to refuse,
he walked her home;

promised to sit with her
at the Saturday game.

They met at half past,
walked with the crowd

to the grassy goal end,
bumping shoulders

just a little too often.
If he had to kiss her

it would be his first.
At half time he heard

her whisper low
he loves me / he loves me not.

Surprised, he leaned in,
then saw her bitten fingers

slowly pulling the legs
from a living spider.

Arm's Length

I'd like to be
an octopus
with one shy
and one bold
arm. They say
each arm has a
separate role –
can get in touch
without involving
the brain. So,
right arm of mine,
the bold one,
reach out now
for my would-be
lover's hand.
And left arm,
ah look,
you're blushing.

Surprising Material

Hard until it meets your mouth –
thanks to the body's latent heat,
turns from solid to liquid,
becomes itself.

This change from tropical
rainforest nut of cocoa bean
to a wild bittersweet taste
did not happen overnight,

did not happen by accident.
Scientists tested whether
the effects of chocolate
last longer than kissing.

They do.

Border Bus 1979

Southbound from Belfast I feel a physical shift before Carrickarnon.
Knees tightening, hands snatching handbags, knuckles whitening.
Matches are struck, cigarettes sucked.

We speed up before we slow down.

I don't have a VCR stashed in a washing powder box in the hold
or whiskey in lemonade bottles hiding in a Santa sack –
but I know others do, making smugglers of us all.

The customs men board, pick on a few football holdalls,
search one oddly shaped Woolworths bag. Seem satisfied.
They go out to check around the back.

Across the aisle a white South African father and son chat,
What are they doing, Dad?
I'll bet they're looking in the luggage compartments…

Now, hardly a word spoken. Locked in our local moment.
The persistent cougher miraculously cured.
Behind me, knitting needles click, click, click.

Finally, a slam of locks and voices rise.
The engine revs, indicator lights blink on.
Relief slowdrips down steaming windows.

Dad? comes the kid's voice,
Did they find any blacks?

The Focus Puller's Father

While others search for hats and coats,
we wait as final credits roll.

Best Boy, Gaffer, Key Grip,
words which have criss-crossed

our dinner table for months
like so many camera angles –

we know all about Dolly tracks,
windsocks and pulleys.

By 10 you'd become expert
at guessing distance – a human

measuring tape, practising on the cat.
You watched how people in cafes

leaned forward as they spoke.
Now, you don't look through the lens,

but you have the most vital task
– to keep that image sharp.

Here comes your name,
tears blur my eyes.

At Sadler's Wells Stage Door, London

Minutes since applause,
still sweating,
orchestra members exit,
– Stravinsky's
Rite of Spring all done.
Many sign out in silence,
their collective bubble
of music making
vaporising.

Two together now,
say *Enjoy the break,*
as the violas pass.
Almost jolly, the double bass
player leaves alone,
clutching his instrument
to his chest
like a much loved
blow-up doll.

Vaudeville Talent Night

So come take a look, give me the hook or the ovation
— La Cage aux Folles

Balancing a fishbowl
with Molly fish inside, she juggles;

in a red check suit, the blackfaced
comic spares his own blushes;

a clay modeller attempts the Tour d'Eiffel
and fails. A quartet of singing boys – sing.

Each offered a chance until the crowd
chants *The hook! The hook!*

Waiting in the wings,
curtains striped from sun –

my shepherd's crook necks
the hopefuls, one by one.

Organ Symphony

"I compose, fulfilling the function of my nature,
as an apple tree grows apples."

Saint-Saëns

'The keyboard was very close to his heart,'
hums the late night DJ

and in my demi-sleep
Saint-Saëns' insides

take on new shapes.
Piccolo clavicles

above keyboard ribs.
Lungs a perfect cello,

as veins of violin strings
bring notes to bones

around a French horn gut.
His breath rises and falls

andante to the bass drum
bloodsong of his heart,

while his bronchioles
branch and fruit.

Built-in Adolescence

Adam (35) on the Friday train
boasts he has his lab coat
in a bag for Mam to wash.

An old man griping
about checkout delays
begins to stamp his feet.

Caitlin puts Dolly Mixture
around the edge of the bath
to encourage her husband to bathe.

When I read Emily Brontë
I still wonder if I was adopted
and want to run away.

Desire

On seeing Cage ll – a Paul Seawright photograph

Half two on Saturday, my rusty,
latticed edges leach rain, caged

as I am to this door of a Belfast bar.
I ache for darker, happy hours –

when I turn threshold, my bar
becomes the *Zan-Zi-Bar.*

I yearn for touch, not Sean's rough
shunting of my bolt belt at teatime

but the doorbell pulse of index fingers
on my one spot domino of electricity.

A Broad Vocabulary

Cuboidal and *Columnar,* once my favourite words,
rolled round on my tongue at school.
Under my breath I loved the click
of shamrocked syllables lipped with air.

But when I first heard *Cunnilingus* –
that took the biscuit. Never said out loud,
only as a whisper.

So, when tough but pretty Billy,
snogging me after the roller disco, asked
Do you do any other sort of kissing?
I said *No* like the question was daft.

Way later I twigged he meant *fellatio,*
a rocket of a word I'd not yet heard.

Feeder

It's your first trip to a diner
and it's self service for sparrows.

Your feet tattoo the wood
as you practice bill wiping,

fluffing tiny new feathers
each time your mother lands.

I'm happy to have
trimmed the ash enough

for you two to feed together –
to have set up this roadside café

where you perfect your chirp
and only have eyes for your mother.

Storm Petrel

Little thing, hardly an ounce in my hand –
a feather weight you are, my water witch.

Mitty, some call you or *Walk on Water*,
a follower of Peter, you paddle the sea.

Hated by sailors for your love of slop,
harbinger of lower weather,

you tell of storms to come,
need their wind to fly and feed.

Both insult and compliment,
revolutionary Tom Tailor bird

you fly like a bat, burrow like a mouse
shelter and roost in warm island earth.

Oily enough to be killed, dried, burned
as a candle to light Shetland homes –

you shine still, haunt us,
your call a spooky chattering.

Come Back Peter, Come Back Paul

Once Philip Sparrow
and Wagtail Willy,
lots of Jenny Wrens,
and wakes called Kitti.

Gone Jack Snipe,
stay redbreast Robin,
Many Jack Daws,
Jenny Owl uncommon.

Tom Tit survived,
Poll Parrot died,
in books alone Ralph Raven,
yet Mag stuck to Pie.

Once this desire
for a naming word
opened our hearts
to the Dicky bird.

Nature Table

for Catherine Murphy

Each September
ranged in front of you,
row on row, they settle.

Fuchsia, clover,
loosestrife – boisterous ones
are first to catch your eye –

lily and iris bloom later.
Come Christmas, holly
may scratch and startle.

Months can pass
before shy celandines
raise their hands.

Amongst a class
of busy bulrushes,
the breezes come –

tears or giggles rinsing
to high laughter.
You bring home stories

of mischief and nettle –
pupils and teacher
honeysuckled.

Atlas

Been so long
since you touched me,
my spine tingles
to feel your hand
lift me from the shelf.
Oh, the turn of me
in your fingers.

Don't think I've not seen you,
click online, plan.
Last week you booked
a whole trip
on your phone.
I almost died.

It's not just me –
you reach for
Chambers Dictionary,
he blushes with relief.
Thesaurus worries
her pages are stuck,
Gideon's past caring.

About this box
on the floor –
you caress me,
yet talk of Oxfam
or Attic. Must I leave?

Feel the sun warm me,
my pinks and blues
reminding you that
my world is still yours.

The Sound That Photographs Make

1.

This one, you on O'Connell Bridge
where the photographer caught you unaware,
wind in your hair, full coat skittering –
your face beautiful and young.
A Sinatra song in full fifties swing.

2.

There, posed at yet another stone ruin,
you smile, the road ribboning
silver behind you. We harmonised
to Don McLean in the car,
'By the waters of Babylon.'

3.

Here, a rainbow above Rathfran
spreads its arms around Killala Bay
where your ashes mix with estuary tides.
You rest with the curlews now.
Listen! Their song is everywhere.

An Sruth Geal /
The Bright Stream

Once the main road to Sligo,
now verges encroach, lazy with scutch,
tarmac puddles the same hollows
that bumped our family car

passing each July full of sleeping bags,
sleeping budgie, slobber dog, mewing cat
and five wide-awake children
bursting with holiday hopes.

This may have been the very turn
where one of us triumphed
at *Animal, Vegetable or Mineral*
or spotted our fiftieth Red Cortina.

Both parents now across the Lethe
see how the road still floods
here at Ballinafad bridge;
keeps bright our memory stream.

lost alphabet of gym

X of cartwheel
O of forward roll

A of a lean
against any old wall

X of a sprawl
on sweaty foam mat

after soaring *H*
of a high jump

T of hand stand
feet to fence

Y of my arms
calling for ball –

gone, my hopeless, teenage attempts
to win the heart of Miss Mulhall.

Brownies 1969

Tuesday nights lined up in patrols
Elf, Sprite, Imp and Gnome,
as Owls – Tawny or Grey –
inspected our well knotted ties,
our shiny badges
and neatly rolled berets.
Shoes buffed, socks beige,
we held out spotless hands –
palms up, palms down,
then the weekly command –
About Turn, Forward Down Bend
to check that our knickers were brown.

Look Back

on seeing Degas' "The Dancing Class"

Only when alone would her tongue sharpen,
tear strips off other girls in ballet class.

She was a little bitch, saying no one
could dance half as well as her.

Bunhead, she'd sigh, *feet too fat,
too slow. Look, her neck is dirty!*

By thirteen I'd given up,
sold my pointe shoes half price,

left the new girl a warning: *Try to ignore
that mirror, she really isn't nice.*

My Contagious Sister

for Una

Will you two just stop! and we'd try,
focused on the Sunday roast, peas and potatoes.

But the lure of the laugh, unbridled
as a wild pony, reeled us back in.

I'd glance and you were pure gone,
then so was I – a fit of the giggles rising through

our small bodies – shoulders shaking,
eyes streaming, noses bubbling.

I caught from you, my giggling sister,
an incurable love of laughter.

Face Value

1.

At the wash basin I watched you shaving,
never wanting to miss a minute, my face
level with the basin staring up, as you
pulled faces for a change. Soaping, scraping
with open blade or new-fangled razor,
you dipped and tapped metal to ceramic and back
to jawline again, stretching the skin taut on your neck
until I passed the towel. You patted on cologne,
now smooth and handsome. I looked and looked,
not learning but catching your love of mirrored
self.

2.

You never cared for make-up, never taught us how.
A pink box of powder clouds rarely opened,
dust on all the little pots. Only lipsticks rubbed smooth,
the muted ones, never loud. You had little time
for mirrors, a lick and a spit would do. You brushed
your hair while putting on your shoes, chose your
alternating teacher's dresses like so many uniforms.
And when you did put on your 'war paint'
we teased your dolled-up face. There was no chair
at your dressing table, never time
to sit.

Swinging 60s

I like men real well –
just don't want one of my own:
a pal of my mother's from college
who wore checked slacks
with under the heel elastics,
captained the ladies golf club,
drove a turquoise car around Cork,
teaching housewives to sew and cook.
Years later, one evening with gin,
she said she'd had a fling with my father,
they went to the Venice Festival
for a weekend. It seemed a trifle.
He liked women real well too,
didn't want just one of his own.

Clearing the Lane

in memoriam GB

Severed purple thistles
tangle into living hedge,

snipped rye grass rustles
a thin tune skywards –

while you are dying
I cut brambles, wait for rain.

Grief #1073

We pass a lime green field
just as a foal places
his legs askance,
looks back at the mare

and relieves himself
with a start, as though
still working out
which bits did what.

You say how lovely he is,
how lush his home
with his mother beside him
for a long time to come.

Out of nowhere, after all these years,
my eyes spring quick tears.

Served

Fish was sullen,
mouth closed,
meeting the plate head on.
Potato kept his last eye
on the errant peas,
as ever taking up
too much space.
In the lemon quarter
tension rose
like goosebumps,
before the final squeeze.

Burnaby Park 7.55am

The mainline train halts
just south of the station
waiting for its green light.

The park suddenly busy
with rushed commuters,
a slouch of schoolkids.

Standing midfield
throwing ball for two collies,
I'm jolted back 35 years

when college-bound, I waited
on that packed platform
for the mainline that never came.

Word whispered of a body
on the line at Three Trout River.
Your meticulously chosen moment,

Liam, the village at a standstill.
I turn to look at your family home
still parkside as on that grey day

when your 19-year-old name
was gasped along the platform.
It still clings like dew

to this moment –
to the grass, the railway
and the mainline train.

Timing

When fondness
made his heart
grow absent,
he considered
ways of flight –
how and when
he might reveal
his true intent.
He'd never meant
to keep pretending.
He'd tell her tonight.

But, when in the dark
he went to speak,
she gently touched
his mouth,
So tired honey,
can't it wait?
I really need a
full night's sleep.
Hours before he woke –
the car, dog and woman
were gone.

Light Your Own Fire

The prefrontal cortex, like a conductor waving a baton, urges our brain to hunt for that lost name or date, while we drive cars, or make the dinner. Later, we remember as clearly as July and can't believe we ever forgot it. Take Wag Dodge, a fireman caught in a forest blaze in '49 who, realising he was in danger, stopped, began to burn the grassy area around him, then hunkered down, kerchief to mouth, taking shallow breaths close to ground as the fire passed over. Afterwards, with 13 dead, Wag couldn't explain where his idea came from. He had no memory of learning that trick but somewhere in his head, a conductor was wildly waving.

The End of St. Barbara

Her father understood the three windows
in her new bath house proved her conversion.

    Patron saint of mathematics – pray for us.

He oversaw her torture but the fire snuffed out,
by morning all her wounds had healed.

    Patron saint of extreme events – pray for us.

He beheaded her himself and she swore before dying
that to call her name in distress would bring relief.

    Patron saint of the Italian Navy – pray for us.

Heading home in a thunderstorm,
her father was consumed by flame.

    Patron saint of lightning – pray for us.

In 1969 she was cut from the Litany;
her story judged to be entirely fabulous.

    Patron saint of fireworks – grant us peace.

On Kilburn High Road

A damaged ankle hobbles my walk,
outpaced now by peckhopping pigeons.
A man shuffles past, his wife unkindly
tugs his arm. Coming towards us,
at pace, a young woman, face bruised
and cut, hair loose, dares us to stare.
Further along, an outburst of anger
from a maroon hijab surprises.
The cracked pavements, taunted by litter,
say little. My limping foot, wary
of their rough edges trips me back
to when this thoroughfare was Roman,
a quiet part of Watling St. where up ahead
Boudica took on Paulinus, and lost.

Little Skellig and the Icebergs

Pure black, sharp as pencil lead
I perch with brother Michael off Portmagee
eager for summer when I wear
my white coat of gannet. Nesting begins
in May, each bird the size of a flying tom cat.

They raise their chicks on my shoulders,
filling the air with whirring cries,
coating me guano white. Then come
the boats of tourists and Tomás,
the skipper who loves me more than Michael.

Today he shows me a photo of my arctic cousins –
blue white pinnacles rising from the same ocean,
moving at snail's pace down the coast of Newfoundland,
past Tickle Bay and Come By Chance –
I have never seen anything more beautiful.

Tomás says that if a seabird lands on them,
it means they are grounded on a sand bank
where they will quickly calve and melt.
The boats come, filled with other tourists,
smelling of diesel and dairy.

He would like someday to see these icebergs,
I ask him to take me with him. He says he will.

Jet Dracula[*]

Albert's death
dressed Victoria
black for life –

a silver lining
for Whitby town,
now mining
fossils of monkey puzzle
for gems not fuel –

the dark jewel
of lament and regret
transformed
from mine to throat,
as Stoker would.

[*] In 1890 Bram Stoker visited Whitby
and credited a book he read at the local
library with the origin of his central
character's name.

Settled

You married him then and him a settled man?
I did. He beat me on our wedding day,
said I was only a knacker.
Me da had warned me he was a bad one, called him
'that Dublin fellah.'

And you stayed with him even with the hidings?
I loved him, loved the ground he walked on.
The way I looked at it was,
I'm going to have beautiful children from him.
And I did.

To Make a Mark Not Permanent

Peniccilum(def): a fine brush

Stylus of old Rome,
if I drew a line with you
it would be 35 miles long.

Ever dry, no spilt ink,
your hexagonal shaft
fixes you to table or ear.

Beloved of carpenter,
cartoonist and child,
it's said that Steinbeck

used 60 of you a day
on *Grapes of Wrath*,
300 on *East of Eden*.

Breadcrumbs were always
known to do the trick, yet
stationer, Hyman Lipman

first glued on the rubber –
I think you've always known
your role was to be erased.

Driving Lessons

Driving, I try to get inside
someone else's mind:

my calmer sister
always late, never rushing;

my uncle who cruises
and glides at speed;

or my first boyfriend
who taught me

to never float a corner
but to always drive

right through it –
accelerating on the curve.

I hear a trace of his voice,
saving me ever since.

Grief #8 Endanger

We drove at high speed as if arriving
quicker could help.

You, so recently alive, warm to touch
and so soft. The nurses left us,

we held you 'til the June sun rose,
your hands beginning to chill,

me wrapping them in mine
as if they could be warmed.

Still dawn, I drove to your house
to search for your typewritten note,

your wishes for the days ahead,
a final gift to us all.

Tempting the gods I drove
the wrong way down a one-way road –

the first action of a summer
when being alive seemed unnecessary.

Oh Danny Boy

Home from war
to our lowland town,
and a cottage
cheaply built
for men with eyes
gunpowder grey.

Lost yer marbles?
we mocked, teased
him by whistling
that tune every day,
copied his limp,
gave no peace.

His body found
on the winter bog,
ditch-hunkered,
using his crutch
as a rifle –
taking aim.

Air Brakes

Arthur patrols Whitshed Road,
a tiny man in a soiled beige coat.

Driving his imaginary car, he pauses
to close every open gate.

Bandy in his walk, countless times a day
he raises that handbrake, lets it off with a sigh.

May Delaney

Your elbows deep in suds, pumping
smoother than an uilleann piper,

kneading our clothes of seven sizes,
rubbing cloth on cloth so hard.

Lux flakes becoming airborne.
A scent so clean fills the back kitchen

as you heave those snakelike
shapes onto the draining board

before rinsing and wringing begin.
I watch you wrestle, dip and twist,

your arms pinked by heat, hands somehow
stronger in water, wedding ring never off.

Too small to help – I wish I'd told you,
Mrs D, that you were magnificent.

Playground

Plastic seats, blue, red and green
swing of their own accord
in squally April rain – childless,
making their own fun.

Missing Words

for Shirley McClure

The day has come
to write the poem
you urged me to –
about the lack
of a word
for the spoon,
fork or knife
left in the basin
when the water's
poured out.

Since you left,
I've been busy
collecting lists
of other gaps,
like when socks
get spin-sucked into
the duvet cover
or how starlings
sound down the
chimney. There
should be a
word for that.

So now
I'm ready.
I'm just going to
finish these dishes
and I'm straight
away off to the desk.
I tip out the water,
see nothing
left behind.

Underfoot, Your Bed of Peel

Dimple skinned sun, I juggle you,
ball of juice, your waxy rind

firm and thudding. Itch of pedicel
on my palms as your stalk turns.

Peeling dizzies you, my fingers deft
but cautious, afraid to dig right through.

Skin drops to concrete floor,
tang rises as others imitate.

Pith revealed, an almost shiver,
your destiny always to be here, half time

at this football game in Brady's Field.
I segment you, make sphere a memory,

slot half moons into my mouth,
tiny sacs explode – sweet, sharp, over.

Unshackled

In my teens I grew like ivy,
wriggling for room,
spilling from girdled stem,
seeking only the next stone
to latch onto. Years
'til I paused and saw you
grow toward me ever closer,

your leaves a brilliant green,
roots less pot-bound.
We began our winding lives
the day I knew I'd been suckered
into looking for stone
when I should have
been reaching for air.

A Collie Called Beamish

And what can you teach me
as you chase, collect, return

this ball to my feet? My move –
I throw. Your tail flagwaving,

salmon tongue lengthening,
you race up the dunes to catch.

Then, a sudden dash to sea, dip
for a moment, your choice.

You gallop back otter-quick,
pausing only to shake.

Come to my arms, my Beamish boy,
what can I learn but joy?

Joy comes to me as
a Flying Trapeze

I close my eyes and feel myself
swing high in the big top,

corner to corner, gripping
tightly to the narrow bar,

I swoop down, arc back,
soar to the top and leap –

twisting to meet waiting hands
chalk wristed, always upside down.

In my secret high wire life
the faceless catcher never misses.

EITHNE HAND grew up in Greystones, Co.Wicklow and is a writer and producer. *Fox Trousers* is her first poetry collection. She studied Religion and English at Mater Dei Institute, and Journalism at DCU before working fulltime in RTÉ TV and Radio for twenty years until 2007. She has written and directed three radio plays broadcast on RTÉ Radio 1 and her documentary, *Voicejazz*, won a Prix Italia for Best Work on Music. She was Head of RTÉ Radio 1 from 2003 to 2006 and now works independently with RTÉ lyric fm on its weekly poetry feature, *Poetryfile*. She worked with Gay Byrne for the final four years of his *Sunday Jazz* programme. As a theatre producer, she tours the one man shows *The Man In The Woman's Shoes* and *I Hear You and Rejoice*, both written and performed by Mikel Murfi. From 2014 to 2017 Eithne was the curator of the First Thought strand of the Galway International Arts Festival. She spends her time between Greystones and Ballinafad, Co Sligo.

salmonpoetry

Cliffs of Moher, County Clare, Ireland

"Like the sea-run Steelhead salmon that
thrashes upstream to its spawning ground,
then instead of dying, returns to the sea—
Salmon Poetry Press brings precious cargo to
both Ireland and America in the poetry it
publishes, then carries that select work to its
readership against incalculable odds."

TESS GALLAGHER

The Salmon Bookshop
& Literary Centre

Ennistymon, County Clare, Ireland

"Another wonderful Clare outlet."
The Irish Times, 35 Best Independent Bookshops